IMPORTANT PARTS

A Coloring Book for the Crotch Enthusiast

This book is for anyone with a crotch. There are cock-n-balls and vajayjays all over it, so a good sense of humor will really help you enjoy your coloring time. I hope that if, perhaps, you've had a challenging relationship with your own crotch, this book will lead you toward a place that feels a little safer and a little happier. Know that these pages are loaded with love, as well as with a recognition that body stuff can sometimes be hard.

On these pages you'll see various genitals represented by very rudimentary drawings. I did this to emphasize the basic components of genital anatomy so that you can find parallels on your own body (if you haven't already). I work in pelvic health... I've explained this stuff a lot and know that for various reasons, it can be difficult. For this reason, I included non-gendered name suggestions and a drawing guide so you can customize your very own crotch doodle!

Don't put limits on how you think about or represent your crotch. You may have a vulva but feel like your "psychic cock" is also beautifully represented by one of these images (or vice versa). There's no need to fit into a constructed category. Enjoy and explore your body for the limitless possibilities and rich pleasure that it holds.

When you color one that you're really proud of, tag me on instagram with **#crotchenthusiast**.

Enjoy!!

Heather

Anatomy

Everyone has the same basic bits whether they're assigned male or female at birth, whether or not they have an intersex body variation, or whether they've undergone hormonal or surgical genital changes. Our parts are just arranged differently and are amazingly varied from one person to another! While we are free to call them anything we like, finding some standard words for our anatomy that feel good (or at least acceptable) can be handy if we need to describe a concern to a healthcare provider.

Here are a few terms that might work for you:

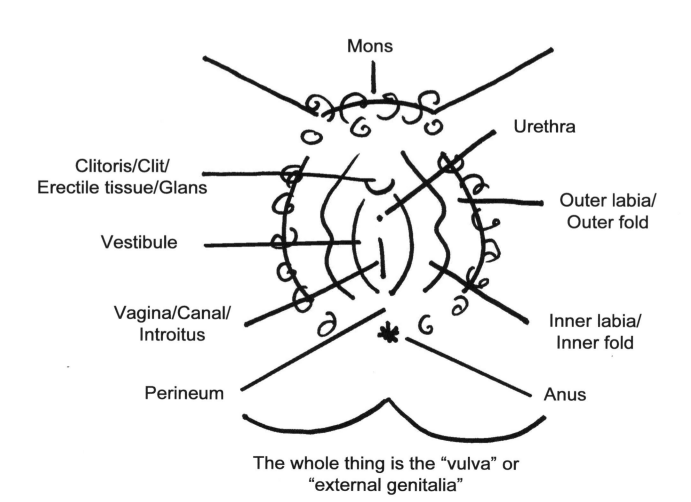

Mons

Urethra

Clitoris/Clit/
Erectile tissue/Glans

Outer labia/
Outer fold

Vestibule

Vagina/Canal/
Introitus

Inner labia/
Inner fold

Perineum

Anus

The whole thing is the "vulva" or
"external genitalia"

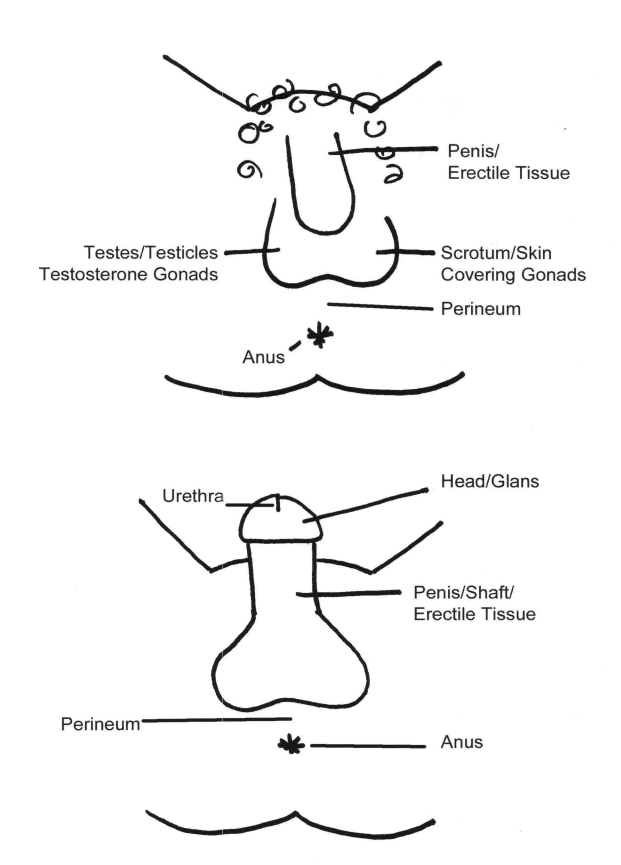

Penis/
Erectile Tissue

Testes/Testicles
Testosterone Gonads

Scrotum/Skin
Covering Gonads

Perineum

Anus

Head/Glans

Urethra

Penis/Shaft/
Erectile Tissue

Perineum

Anus

Drawing Lesson

If words alone are either too hard or not enough, you can also learn to draw a quick sketch of how you want your parts represented. That way you can point to what you want to discuss. In addition to being a valuable tool for communicating with healthcare providers, this can be be really useful in important or awkward (or both!) conversations with sexual partners.

Here's a simple guide to drawing your parts. Feel free to modify it for whatever feels right to you. There are SO MANY ways you can draw genitals!

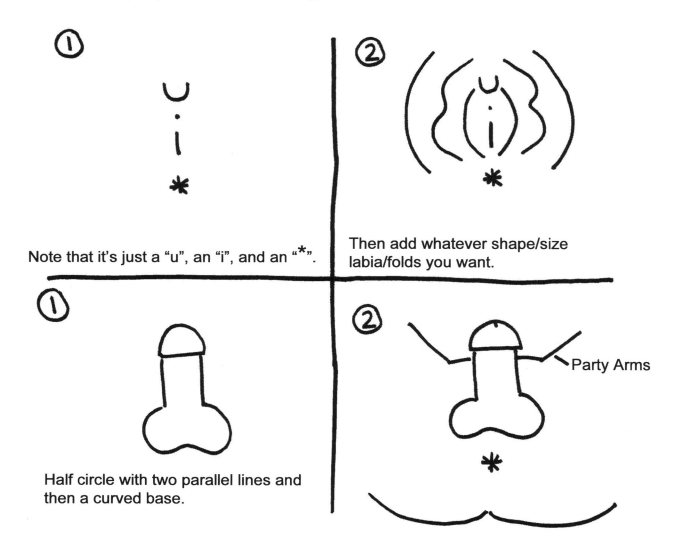

Note that it's just a "u", an "i", and an "*".

Then add whatever shape/size labia/folds you want.

Half circle with two parallel lines and then a curved base.

Party Arms

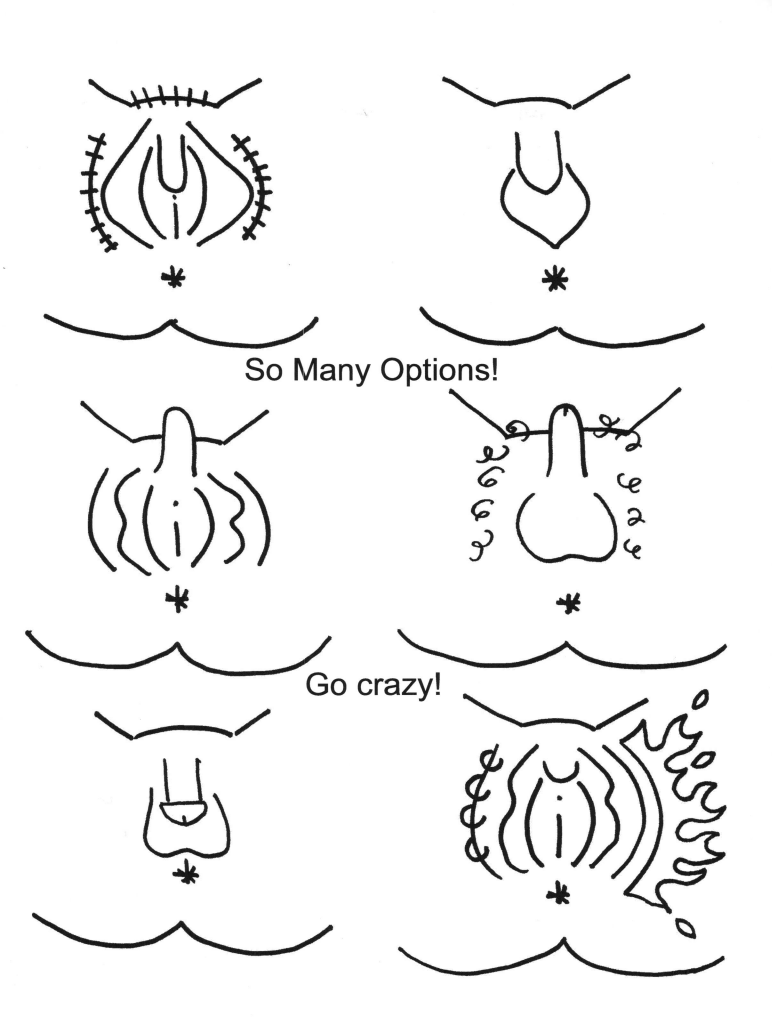

So Many Options!

Go crazy!

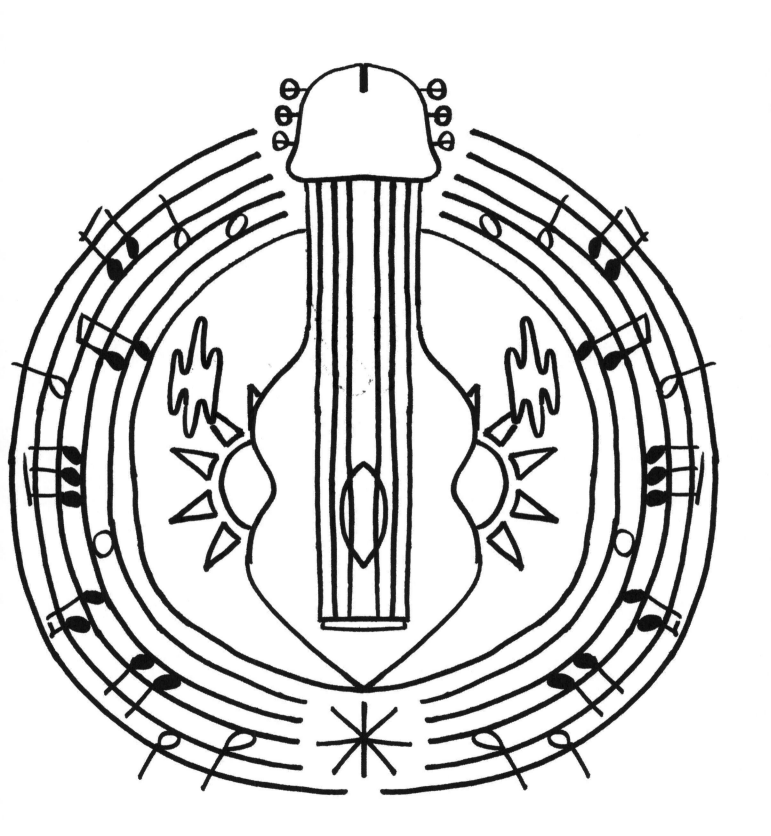

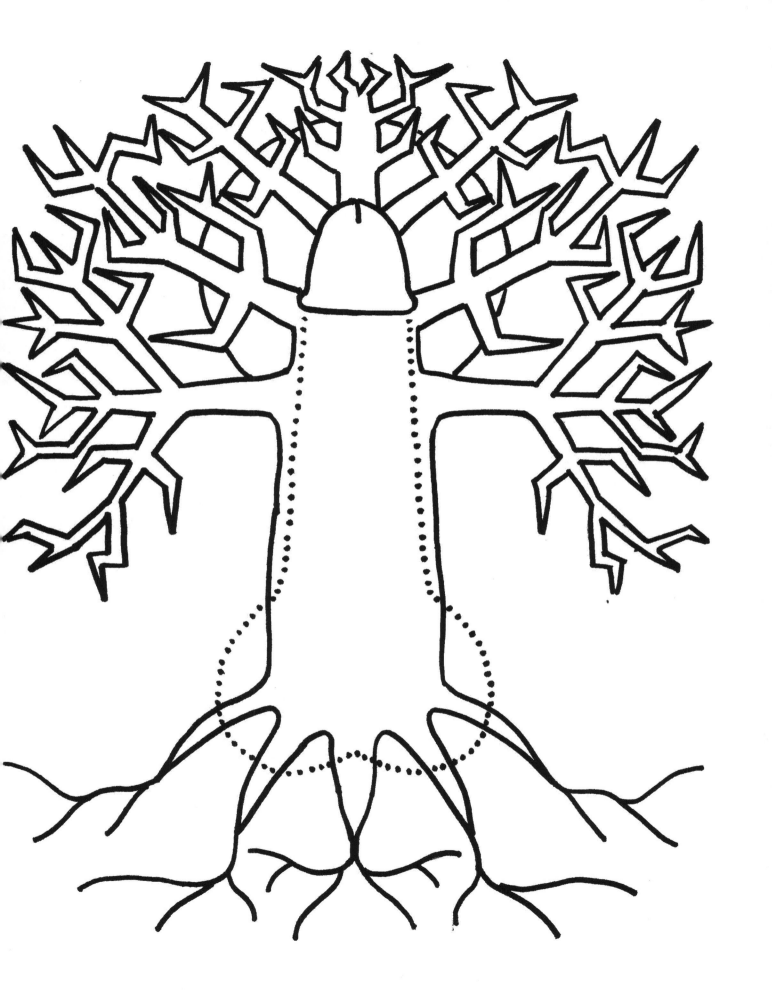

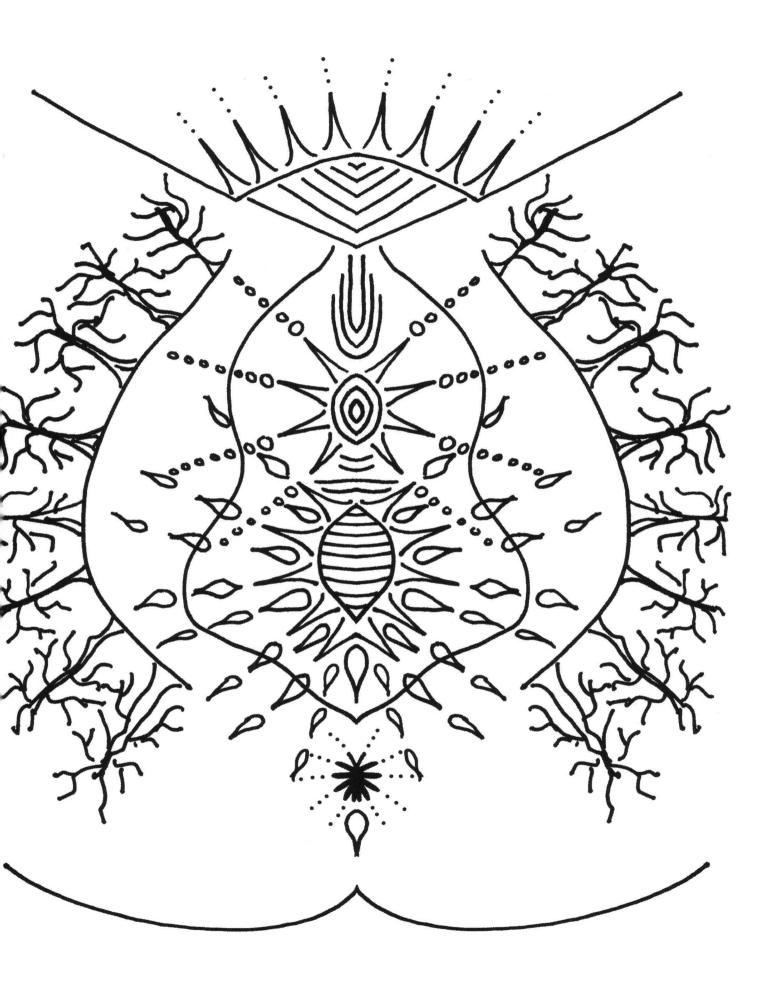

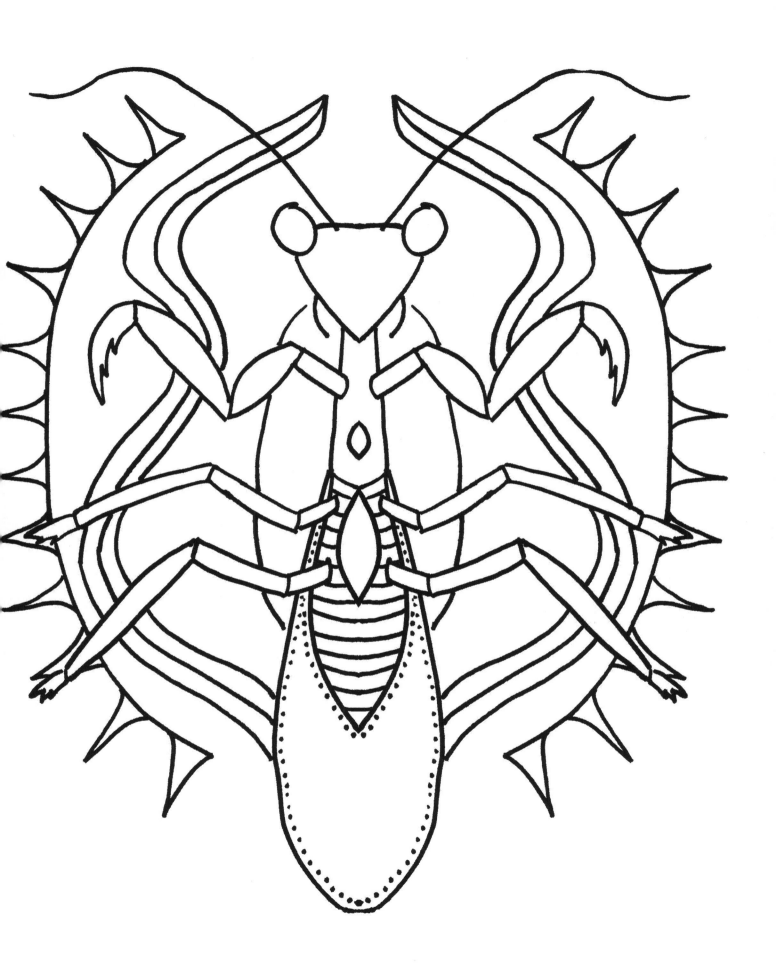

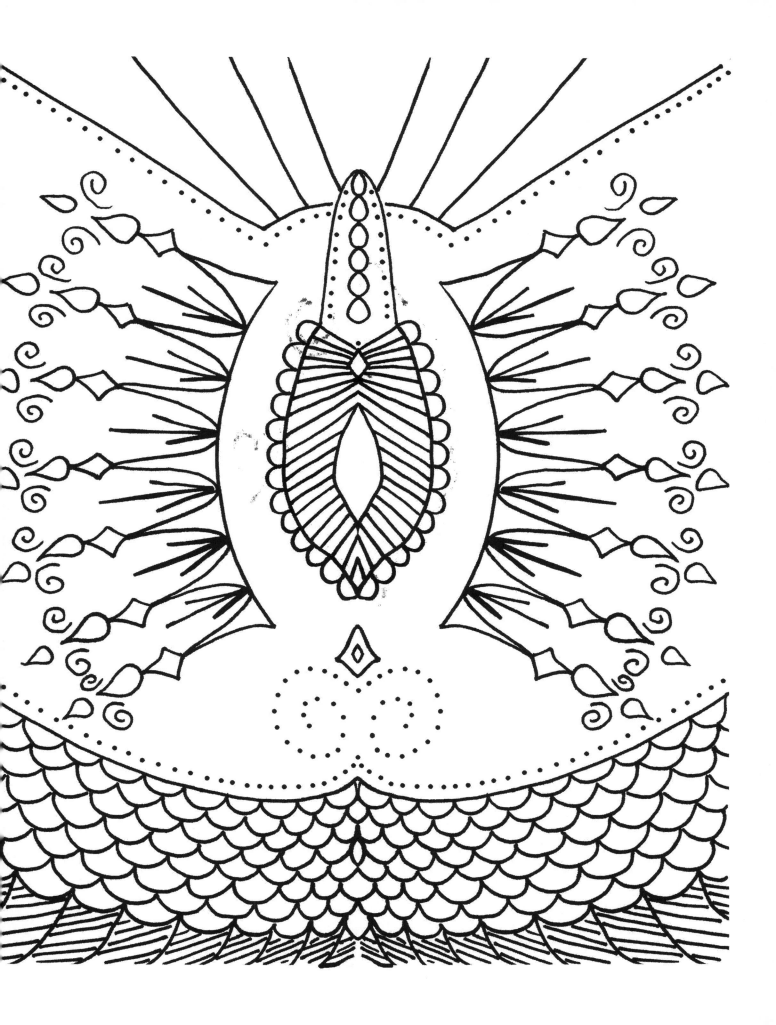

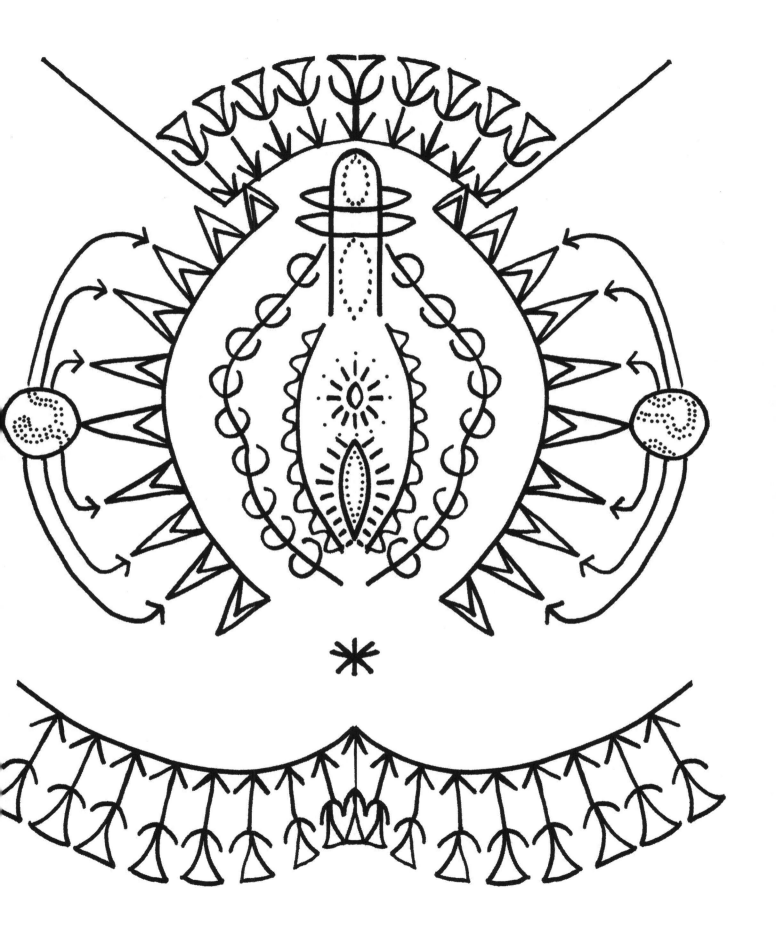

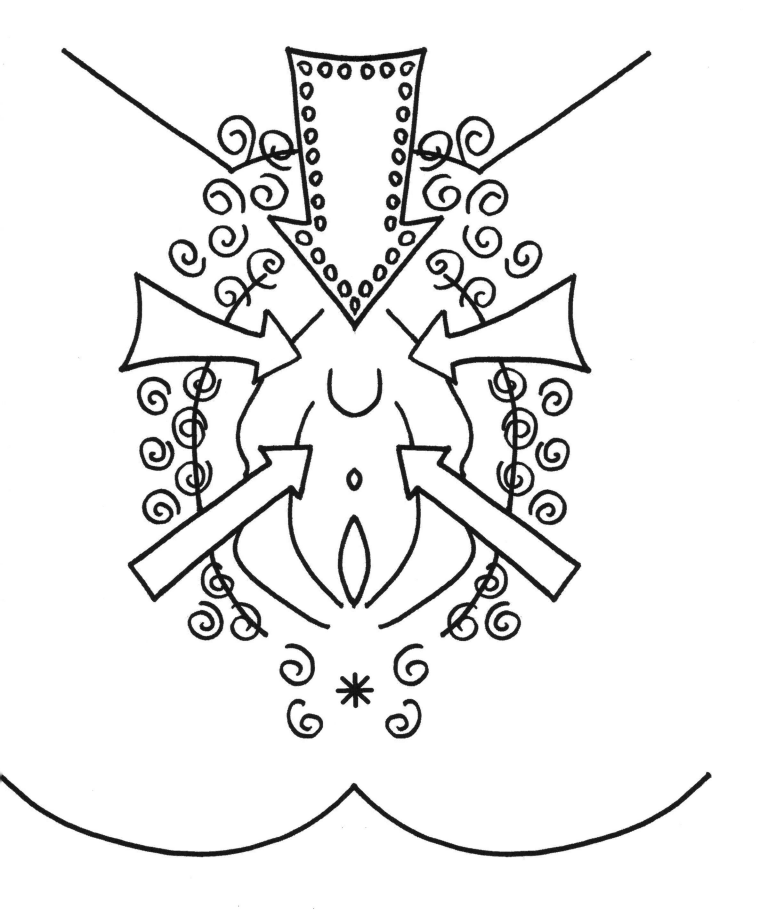

VINO & VULVAS™

edgy
inclusive
informative

Thank you for your support!!

If you'd like to purchase more books,
or find some of these designs on shirts,
mugs, notebooks, and other goodies,
go to www.vinoandvulvas.com and
click on SHOP.

Vino & Vulvas meets monthly in
Asheville, NC. Tickets and event
information are on the website,
and you can follow us on Facebook:
www.facebook.com/vinoandvulvas.

If you color a picture you're really proud of,
please post it to Instagram with
#crotchenthusiast.

Made in the USA
San Bernardino, CA
12 November 2019